Soul Purpose

ANTHOLOGY OF FREE VERSE POETRY

JESSICA MACHAN

DEDICATION

I dedicate this book to my intelligent and beautiful daughters, who light up everything within my world and have given my life true purpose and meaning. I love you both so much. I also dedicate this book to my friends who have stood by me and offered me support, love and care through my hardest days. I finally dedicate this book to you, my dear reader, and to all who have struggled to reconcile a sensitive soul in a broken world.

All my love,

Jess

TABLE OF CONTENTS

ONE.

IN MY HEAD

i.

Laying here

wondering

if this lingering

sadness

is a life sentence.

It's made me

an inmate

of my mind

and I find myself

spending hours

plotting

my escape.

ii.

Feel it

they tell me.

Don't repress.

Unleash the mess.

Yet once

the floodgates open

I cannot stop them,

and the

outpouring

is so powerful

it tears through my sanity

and rips my

heart to pieces.

So I'm left

broken.

Bruised.

Bloody.

Collapsed inside.

Exposing the weight

of it all for them,

and I feel

everything.

iii.

I sunk

further and further

into the depths of darkness,

as if a weight

had pulled me

deep under

this ocean of pain.

The light

glittering above me

on top of the waves

grew smaller and smaller

and how lonely

it felt

beneath it all.

iv.

I've always felt I was

on the outside of it all:

family,

friends,

coworkers,

communities.

As if rejection,

like my shadow,

never

left.

v.

My reflection

is both

my most hated enemy

and

my dearest old friend.

vi.
So many dreams
I have yet to fulfill;
Please, I am not
ready to go yet.
Pleading with my
mind, I provide
a list of reasons
for us to stay.
Let's stay for my girls.
Let's stay for oceans.
Let's stay to explore
this boundless world.
Let's stay to feel the
cool breeze on our skin
and the sun warming
our face.
Let's stay for friends
and stay for
love.
So many dreams
I have yet to fulfill.
No, I am not
ready to go yet.
Please let us stay,
for us.

vii.

Help.

Four letters.

One word.

One syllable.

And yet the outcry of this single word

builds so intensely in the roots

of my being,

climbing my body

from the bottoms of my feet,

violently grabbing and pulling its

way up towards my mouth,

begging my voice to bellow it out

to any who may listen. *Help*.

I break the silence.

Help.

viii.

My eyes dissect her
bit-by-bit
with a critical stare
I start to add them up.
One becomes two becomes ten
becomes countless.
A collection of flaws.
These critical eyes
grow hot from tears.
How could anyone see
beauty in me?
The mirror stares back
relentlessly
as if to coyly challenge
me to see it
in myself.
As if she accepts I can
let go of these
misbeliefs.
I turn my back abruptly
to avoid it.
Aware that one day
I need to accept her.
One day
I need to love her.

ix.

Time seems to slowly creep by

when my mood runs low.

The seconds ticking

one-by-one,

as I sit in quiet

and count moments,

then breaths.

Senses slow along with it,

as if every noise mutes,

every smell fades,

every touch softens,

while time

inches

on.

x.

Pain is all too familiar,

I somehow

seem to find comfort

in its arms.

xi.

How ambiguous

faith has become,

my beliefs now lie

in my will and yours.

xii.

It begins to bubble over,
like hot lava melting its way
down a volcanic mountain
while dark clouds of ash
grey the sky above.
An unstoppable force
that eradicates everything
which dares stay close enough
to suffer the sting
of her vengeance.
Even she herself cannot stop it.
The flashing in her eyes
serves as a sanction
for the tears she cries,
and the world bares the penalty.
Though she lay dormant
for a time, this eruption
of fire and smoke,
this predictable implosion
has left her
barren to the core.
Years may pass
before her rebirth.

xiii.

You were there.

With your greedy hands

on my body and though

I barely remember,

my stomach turns at

the thought.

You were there.

My mind was not.

It escaped once

again, to keep itself

safe.

You were there.

I was

not.

xiv.

I fill it with pain.

I fill it with tears.

As it pours out

from within.

Exposed I fall onto paper,

the ink will not let me hide.

It charges into battle.

Courageous, it is

my knight.

It will fight for me,

for you.

xv.

What a curse it can be

to see the good in people,

for so many will

exhibit their light,

only to engulf me

in their darkness.

xvi.

When I thought it had left

how suddenly

it returns.

The tightness in my throat.

The burning in my chest.

The gasping for oxygen

as if my body

cannot get enough,

and I fight every tear

as they flood my cheeks.

All the emotions

I had so neatly buried

rise up again

and I am lost

within them.

xvii.

I sit in silence on my bed,

my mind racing

while my body remains still.

Thoughts overpowering,

emotions escalating

and yet,

surrounded by quiet.

Gentle humming in the distance,

my furnace warming

my cozy home,

plant leaves swaying from the air.

And me,

sitting in silence on my bed,

wishing my

mind would slow,

the knots would release

in my belly,

the panic would ease

in my heart.

Please I beg,

I only want peace.

Peace of mind.

Of heart.

Peace.

xviii.

And I'm drowning

in it.

Gasping for air,

it's not there.

So my lungs fill

only with pain.

It crawls into every

crevice

of my body,

sinking into my chest,

tightly wrapping

my heart

and I can't breathe.

Can't breathe.

The pain,

it's made a home

of me,

which I cannot

escape.

xix.

Smoke,

burning my eyes.

As I feel my body

lighting up in flames.

Yet nothing is there.

Anxiety.

xx.

What do you do

when letting go feels like

your lungs are filling with water,

a personal hell growing hotter

with every minute that passes?

What do you do

when you can't breathe and

you're drowning in this hellish misery,

and the only way out is to

call death to your front door

as a visitor to come offer freedom

from the ache?

And so if I let go

you'll know,

for when you search

for me once again,

I'll be unfindable,

missing,

yet six feet below you.

Where perhaps

I'll finally be free.

xxi.

Nothing can match it.

Nothing can stop it.

As it burns much

too deeply.

The anger you see inside of her

will destroy homes

you built,

then repaired,

and built again.

Why is it so dark? you ask,

Why? Stop.

Yet this force churns,

created from unfounded fear

and lights a blaze

so powerful

it torches everything

around her.

Collapsing on the floor,

heat bleeding from my pores.

The blaze ruins

me too.

xxii.

Please tell me how

my soul

became this

hollow log,

somehow

rotting

from the inside out.

Please tell me how

my heart

became so

blackened,

torturing me

day in and out.

My soul and heart,

this wicked pair,

will not let

me rest.

xxiii.

All my life I've endured

living inside of my head,

how earnestly I wish to step outside of it,

to explore freedom from thoughts.

xxiv.

How my mind is like a hurricane,

fierce, destructive, relentless.

I am forever waiting

for the calm after her storm.

xxv.

Maybe today

wasn't about the light

or the holding on.

Maybe today

was about sitting

in darkness

and listening

to nothing

and feeling

only nothing.

Maybe today

all my mind could do

was power down

and allow me

to breathe.

xxvi.

There are days

when I can carry all of it,

this weight that hangs so heavily

on my shoulders.

There are days

when I barely feel it at all.

As if I've become so strong

it's feather light.

Yet there are days

when I collapse underneath

these burdens that

torture my soul.

These are the days

I slip away inside myself

in order to heal and rise

once again.

TWO.

CULT AND FAMILY

xxvii.

Leaving people I love behind

does not come naturally,

yet I've reluctantly mastered

the skill.

xxviii.

We are all here,

made by two.

Whatever the circumstance.

Whatever the reason.

However, the saddest part of

some creation stories,

is those two may

never know

you.

xxix.

Here it comes,

familiar as before.

You smother

my happiness.

You lay waste

to my joy.

Stomping and beating

it down,

like innocent

blades of grass,

now withered and crushed.

This tearful burning

heats up.

My eyes, they fill with it.

Clenching.

Reminding.

Don't ever forget,

this is what's

real.

Your mind, it lies.

Wake up.

xxx.

Did you hear me mama?

When the tears would flow at night?

I heard yours mama

and I tried to make it right.

Did you miss me mama?

When you wouldn't speak to me?

I only wanted freedom

for my girls and for me.

How did you reconcile it mama?

Pretending we don't exist?

You know it broke my heart mama,

to be so coldly dismissed.

Funny isn't it mama?

Now I'm a mother too,

yet I could never bring myself

to do the things you do.

xxxi.

Was he ever really there?

The memories

are faded now.

His face is foreign,

like a man I've

never met.

His voice is of a stranger,

one who

I struggle to

recognise.

What choices meant more

to him?

The high. The buzz.

They numbed his pain.

And yet,

in the arms of a child

can you not

battle demons?

And in the eyes of a child

you could have

been a hero,

for all she wanted

was a father.

She only wanted

you.

xxxii.
Knock knock,
and there they are again.
Like the Devil hidden
behind kind smiles and
words of eternal hope.
They'll salivate for your soul as you
stop to carefully listen.
Welcoming evil into
your homes,
unknowingly inviting their
judgement.
Their future of destruction
has become yours.
They'll coat your doubts
with words like warm honey
as it sticks and dries
to your soul.
You cannot scrub it off,
it's part of you now.
Threats of loss soon
ring in your ears
and you'll feel like there
is no way out.
Be warned my loves.
Be warned.

xxxiii.

The light gets brighter, you say

anytime you make a change

to your doctrine to suit your needs.

How indecisive your god must be

to never know how

to make up his mind.

Like sheep they will follow you blindly,

stumbling over your

failed prophecies,

and you know very well you've led them astray.

What awaits those who deceive and lie?

Who hold the blood of millions in their hands?

The day will come when you meet your karmic end,

justice shall be served,

and this time you'll be the ones

requiring repentance.

xxxiv.

The heaviest loss

I've ever encountered,

is grieving for those I love

prior to any death.

xxxv.

Everything stood still
in that moment
when I sleepily crept down the stairs
then found you there on the floor.
Frozen in disbelief
my voice eluded me
as my mind feebly attempted
to process what I saw.
A jug of milk or juice,
I cannot remember now,
laying next to your open hand.
And you were still. So still.
The fridge door hung open
as if you left so suddenly. So abruptly.
There was no peace in it.
No silent drifting away in your bed.
An instantaneous exit which left
me, a child, unable to cope.
Your chest doesn't move.
Your eyes do not open.
Your skin pale and colorless.
For mere seconds I observe you
yet felt as if hours had passed by.
I race to my mother's bedroom
but the words will not come,
only desperate sobs fill the silence.
You were gone.

xxxvi.

These blue eyes shine
just as before,
the life in them burns
bright.

Yet you mumble curses
of imminent death,
She's with the devil now,
and I cry.

Do demons cry tears so
pure and heavy?
Can they understand
this loss of family?

They've not just shut
the door:
it's locked, bolted and
forbidden.

I am alone.

xxxvii.

It almost ended for you,

my life.

I struggled but then

decided

the emptiness was all

I knew.

I wanted to break free.

So I chose.

I chose that bottle,

I chose that box,

then water rained them down.

Yet something stirred,

restless,

and the air inside me fought

for more.

So I turned myself in,

and they saved it all,

what was left.

The demons they crawled

the walls that night,

for death I cheated.

I woke.

xxxviii.
In those days her smile
could light up my world.
The joy in her
laughter wound up joy
in my heart so tightly
that no one could
unravel it.
How gently her hands would
run through my hair,
as if the energy
of acceptance and
unconditional love
passed through them.
And when her tears fell,
they would rip a hole
inside of me,
so I would run to her
to save her,
to be her heroine.
But it is no more.
She is gone,
although not far away.
The daughter I am
has become nothing
but a let down.

xxxix.

As I recited your scripture,

I looked up at you

and you down

at me.

Repentance is not an easy thing

when men cannot

sit in your company.

How horrible

you are,

the depravity of your

existence

is so great,

they owe you no

explanation.

You are less.

They are more.

This god-given right

to take my

world away,

and with the

solemnness of a

funeral,

I am dead

to them.

xl.

Your voice arose

out of the dark

depths within you.

You climbed so high,

that table created a giant

and rage enveloped you.

Your words

shot like arrows

into the chests of those

who stood by.

I could not save you.

How deeply your

feet bled that day.

How hellish the fire

burned in your eyes.

How can I calm

this monster

that has claimed you?

xli.

This one is damaged,

they sneer,

Don't settle;

she is not the one you want.

Look around you,

how many there are,

take your pick, but

not her.

Can't you see them,

her flaws?

Don't they make you

want to avert

your gaze

from the sin inside of her?

Oh no, she

is not right

for you.

Outnumbered, they say.

Pick any you want.

Leave her behind.

She is nothing.

xlii.
As I filled my lungs
with air
I felt anticipation
to be placed
under the waves
and arise
as somehow more.
Oh, how I longed to
feel you.
My mind racing,
the moment
was here.
As they pulled me
to the surface,
I am his.

Yet he
was nowhere
to be found.

xliii.

What happens to the children

who were never shown love?

Who were not given a voice

or allowed to be heard?

What happens to the children

who were raised on fear?

When their god was never

satisfied with any work?

What happens to the children

who weren't allowed friends?

Who were not guided into

confidence or self-love?

My sweet ones,

immerse yourself

in the love you needed.

Be your own parent.

Radically accept yourself

and indulge in the freedom

of making your own choices.

I see you, sweet child.

I hear you.

I love you.

xliv.

Is it true?

Souls burn there?

Fire rises up around them?

Pitiful screams?

Forever in pain?

Forgotten?

Suffering endlessly

for sin?

But tell me,

are we not

already there?

xlv.

Guilty is not sufficient

when my insides

turn out

and I erase all

thoughts

as the hurt tears

through me.

He was left, just him

to fend;

why didn't I go back?

He needed

that.

Oh, the mountains I

should have moved

and the skies

I should have

painted

for him.

Years have flown

and I offer

empty hands

if he will

only take

them.

xlvi.

As the years pass by

my goodbyes pile up,

leaving behind a mass grave

of those I used to love.

THREE.

BROKEN HEART

xlvii.
Was it wrong of me
to place it
so neatly for you?
My heart on
this gleaming platter?
You took a bite.
How delicious it
felt to see
you consume
part of me just
even for that moment.
To see me
drip from your lips.
Willing, I offer more,
I give you
all of me.
Chew every part,
I beg.
But you've
had your fill
and my heart has
holes.
So you float to
the next;
hers is still beating.

xlviii.

And I will paint over

your memories

with all the colours

of the morning sky,

so whenever

you try to slip back

into my mind,

a sunrise instead

will greet me.

xlix.

For how long

will I need to resist?

Though I feel

the desire

forming in my heart

and I feel the want

on the tips of my fingers.

This yearning.

This fire

whose embers

never fade.

Oh, for how long

will I need

to resist?

1.

How brief.

How fleeting.

And in an instant,

gone.

Your love

was never

truly mine.

I was a stop

on your roadmap.

A pause.

A breath.

And once your lungs

were filled

and mine depleted,

your journey

continued on

without

me.

li.

Shattering so deeply

how do I find the words

to describe

the desperation of a broken heart.

When all you are, and all you've been

to someone

who meant the world to you

has rejected every part of you.

The tears fall into puddles

in my lap,

a waterfall of pain,

dropping onto my sweater,

wetting my skin

and turning cold.

My breath shakes

and I gasp for air

hoping the oxygen will

numb the hurt

inside of me.

Shattered.

lii.

Just friends
—when your laugh echoes
endlessly in my ears,
haunting me nightly
in my dreams.
Just friends
—when the electricity of
our kiss could light a city,
sending shockwaves from
head-to-toe.
Just friends
—when your body has melted
in its entirety into mine,
weaving our skin
into one flesh.
Just friends
—when your lips once uttered
I love you and the sound
of those words
filled my soul.

Just friends
—no my darling,
for we shall never be.

liii.

I die a little more for you

each time you say nothing.

God this pain, if you knew

how much it hurt

would it change your mind?

Like a cancer, it eats away

at all of the best parts of me

until I no longer know how to play

your game the same way.

My body is too weakened

and my soul has grown tired.

Like a freight train that's run

out of steam,

slowly evaporating into thin air.

Kill the dream.

The dream I had of what could be

and all I wanted to give you.

It is used up.

Murdered

in cold blood.

Now my ghost is all

that's left

to haunt you.

liv.
I have a wound,
many in fact,
which I keep
hidden as best I can.
But when I met you,
I thought in my
naivety
that you would
save me,
that you would
heal them.
When in fact
all you did
was turn the
knife,
sink it deeper,
and I was left
on the verge
of demise.
I realise now
these wounds can
only be mended
by me.

lv.

Your mouth

left a trail of raging heat

spread over my skin,

and in agony

I am reduced

to ash.

lvi.

While you took me

the tears kept falling,

as your body coursed

through mine.

How you stole me

when I didn't stop you,

but didn't let you.

In that moment

it was the end

of us.

lvii.

I will box up my feelings,

my thoughts and my love.

I will seal it so tight

in hopes it will never escape.

I shall hide it in a corner

in the basement of my heart.

Every year I shall bury it

deeper and deeper underneath

time and memories,

underneath joy and pain.

Still, when the nights

creep up and I am alone,

how easily I seem

to unpack

you.

lviii.

Ironic, how

I feared

falling in love.

Then my heart

made other plans,

and against

better judgement

she gave herself

to you,

only to be torn

into a thousand pieces

by your self-serving

hands.

Now I'm left

with my fear of love

magnified a

million times

over.

lix.

I endeavor

to detach my affection

for you.

Determined, I mercilessly

rip out my heart.

As she lays tormented on the ground

she summons you,

for your name seems to be a spell

cast over her,

one she is unable

to relinquish.

lx.

Silence.

How has this single word become

an enemy that wins every fight?

Silence. Your silence.

The loudest quiet I have ever heard,

one that drowns out all other senses

and leaves me with no choice

but to listen to all your unspoken words.

Your silence has become

deafening and my heart

cannot bear this

punishment

any longer.

lxi.
Emboldened or numbed?
Of those I'm not sure which,
but I swallowed it down
as fast as I could.
You smiled. *Liquid courage* you said,
then closed the door.
So, I sat there,
vulnerable,
on the other side of
that wall.
You felt so far,
but still I wait.
Then all at once he's here,
embracing my body,
stealing my soul.
You watch from safety
as I subject to him,
his hands they hurt,
yet I play my part.
Then he's gone,
you carry me back and
so gently place me
before you and it's done.
I purr for you.
I escape in you.
Until the sun is high
and the bruises exposed.

lxii.
They only want to see
your skin.
Gaze upon your innocence.
Feast upon your flesh.
You dance in front
of them.
They compliment and
offer gifts.
Say they wish their wife
did that.
I let them look and watch,
yet they only see
what I let them see.
All the while I escape
into another universe.
Apart from their gaze,
their wallets and words.
Where I can
be free.
Be me.
Just me.

lxiii.

I collect myself

and shudder,

my mind shrugs,

but he loves you,

it's fine.

Let him use you.

It's just play.

Even though it knows

he won't stay.

The sweat is now cooling.

Goosebumps forming.

Tears welling.

No.

Don't cry.

He loves you.

It's fine.

Wounded I fracture.

I'm fine.

lxiv.
The answer
to all your
uncertainties it seems
is to pull away,
shut down,
be silent,
let go.
And my answer
will no longer be
to cling harder,
express more,
voice my needs,
hold on.
Go, my love.
For what you
are seeking,
was never
me.

lxv.

Another time of

separation,

as if in the absence

of the other

it will solve everything.

Yet that is not how

love works, is it?

Love does not abandon

in a time of need.

Love stays.

Love fights.

Love does not give up

and walk away,

only to return

when it suits.

No. This is not how

love works.

And this is how I know

you've never

loved me.

lxvi.

Do not be so easily swayed

by the opinion of others,

for if our love amounts

to the mere gossip of friends

then it shall not withstand

the tempests of life

which surely will

arise.

Strengthen your resolve,

as will I, and together

we could face it all.

But if mere words can shake

your love for me,

if mere words can cause

you to question,

then my darling,

we do not love

one another

the same.

lxvii.

Today I lit a candle for you;

the flame burned my fingertips.

How fitting, as if it knew

to imitate the burns you

had caused.

I stared at the flame

as it flickered, rose

and fell,

as if it also knew

to imitate the rise

and fall of

our love.

Today I lit a candle for you,

but the flame will

not last.

No, imitating you,

it shall quickly

fade away.

lxviii.

This unavoidable

sickness in my stomach

anytime I contemplate

you with

anyone else.

You are no longer mine,

I should be fine.

Yet I stagger

at the effect

the thought

has on me.

It leaves me crushed

entirely.

lxix.

Reflecting back

what more could I have done?

I worked my heart to the bone

in an effort to be loved by you.

Over before we'd barely begun;

I guess I should have known

I wouldn't be enough for you.

No. There was nothing more

I could have done.

lxx.
My legs were weak
when you said
those words.
My mind lost in you.
Euphoria had
returned,
how desperately
I ached for it.
Yet the pleasure
was only
words,
and the grip you had
me under was short.
But oh how
those words would
crumble mountains
inside of
me.

lxxi.

Could it have been addiction

that kept me

from leaving,

handcuffing me to your love?

Passively keeping me

from pursuing my needs

as I gave you

everything

you asked for?

How could I love

myself so little?

How could I betray

my own heart?

Like rehab

I will cleanse

me of you.

Rest,

repair, now

grow.

lxxii.

Pondering over it all

as I often do,

I find I've grown tired

of crying over you.

Reassurances that

I am in love

no longer ease it,

it is enough.

Not impressed

when you do not try.

Listen carefully,

I finally mean it.

Goodbye.

lxxiii.

As I light them,

a thousand branches

ablaze for you.

Smoke thickens.

Crackling.

Churning.

Its fiery torment

feverishly aglow.

The raging light

brightens up the sky,

yet you

like water

extinguish every ember.

Until we stand

alone

in darkness.

lxxiv.

I've forgotten.

Forgotten how it feels to be pursued

by a man with fire in his eyes

that burns only for me.

I've forgotten.

Forgotten how it feels to be cared for

by a man who gives me his time

and unwavering attention.

I've forgotten.

Forgotten how it feels to be held

by a man whose arms keep me safe

and offer protection.

I've forgotten.

Forgotten how it feels to be loved

by a man who would do anything

to simply see me smile.

How sad that I've forgotten,

and how sad

that you helped

me forget.

lxxv.

I had to let it die.

For all those feelings,

all those thoughts

rented every space

in my head,

until there was no

room left for another

tenant—

myself.

lxxvi.

Have no expectations

you say,

as if you were subconsciously preparing me

for the day you'd tire

and walk away.

lxxvii.

I wish the choice was mine

to stop missing you

but my heart stubbornly

will not forget.

lxxviii.

The quiet hush of

the night.

Words loose

like wine.

We do it for

the butterflies

who died

so long ago,

now resurrected

from the dust.

Deceptively dancing

in the dark

where eyes are

not allowed.

lxxix.

How maddening

I find this cycle,

as it's taken

all my energy

to let you go today,

only to wake tomorrow

to let you go again.

lxxx.

You can make me feel like I am

on top of the world,

or

like I live

miles and miles beneath you.

lxxxi.

Ironic how I met you

on Friday the 13th;

I think the universe

understood the nightmare

that would ensue.

lxxxii.

If I can describe life

without you in one word,

I come back to just one.

Quiet.

Everything has quieted.

My phone is quiet.

My days are quiet.

My evenings are quiet.

My home is quiet.

My weekends are quiet.

And in the midst of

this noiseless revolution

of silence,

the only muted echoes I hear

are my thoughts,

ringing reminiscently

of you.

lxxxiii.

Your scent left first.

That was

easy to erase.

Your clothes were

gone and

I felt lighter still.

Your skin no longer

clung to mine

and your

warmth had faded

with it.

So perfect strangers

we became

and how gladly I

accept it.

For all you were

was wrong

and I needed

to erase you.

lxxxiv.

I guess you are

my drug of choice.

I can't seem to

give you up,

and I can never

have enough.

lxxxv.

How careless

you can be

with me,

as if injuring my heart

then leaving me near death

came easily.

lxxxvi.

A single orange flower

that you plucked from the dirt

while the waves crashed into the shore.

Stolen before it was ready,

then casually handed it to me

without a smile.

But that was all I needed

to fill me up with

affection for you,

to make me fall even

more in love.

To send my heart soaring

so high

I thought she'd never find ground.

Oh, but she did.

She found it hard

and fast.

Now all that's left is the

fading memory of that

single orange flower.

lxxxvii.

Why does my heart

want to fill every page, every line

with you?

She aches but still will not give up,

as if she knows that pouring it all

onto paper will somehow bring you back.

Oh, how she longs for you to come back.

lxxxviii.

I'll build my walls,

this time they'll be higher, stronger,

greater.

Unconquerable.

This time no one shall even

dare try.

Like an insurmountable

mountain,

jaded, sharp, reaching high

into the clouds.

A no man's land

and they'll shudder before her.

Fearful. Intimidated.

Within her I will stay.

Protecting my most sacred treasure,

who has barely gotten out alive,

beating slower than ever,

my heart.

Safe within this fortress

we will stay.

Secure. Sheltered.

Impregnable.

Out of harm's way.

lxxxix.

Steadily comes the night,

darkness paints the sky.

Something is not right,

as I lay alone without you.

Empty bed.

Empty arms.

Empty.

Longing for something

to fill this void,

lonely is the hardest place to be.

Something is not right.

I came home alone without you.

Empty room.

Empty arms.

Empty.

xc.

And suddenly you were gone,

and my entire world

that felt so big,

became so small,

that I began

to suffocate

within it.

xci.

Funny how ready I am

to jump back into the flames

of your love,

which burned me alive

once before.

xcii.

I collapse into pieces

each new time you hurt me

this puzzle

keeps getting

harder and harder

to put back together

again.

xciii.

Sleep evades

as my tired eyes

remain open

and you will not

take leave

from my mind.

It resists

all attempts

to shut down

as it keeps you

incessantly on repeat

all night.

Weakened,

I submissively

surrender.

xciv.

Years I've spent

searching for a semblance

of what could be my

home.

Years I've spent

hoping to have found it

in so many hearts,

but all I found was emptiness.

The years have brought me

to today.

The lessons hurt,

aching yet alone again.

Here you stand before me now.

Could it be?

Is it you?

Or will my home

forever remain

a mystery.

xcv.

And for a moment,

a single blissful moment,

I can see the love

shining in your eyes.

Breaking the constant silence

of you

burying your feelings

beneath you.

Starving I accept it

with open hands and an open heart.

Consuming it purposefully,

greedily,

yet slowly.

Until a breadcrumb of your love

feeds me

once more.

xcvi.

Quivering.

Silent.

Alone.

My heart hangs heavy

as if

her fingertips

are losing their grip

on the edge

of love.

Of life.

Of you.

I breathe fresh air

into my lungs

to invigorate her,

yet she plummets

and I with her.

Why couldn't you

have been

my soft place

to land?

xcvii.

I try to smile as they ask

me the same questions

the others all had.

Sitting across the table

I pay close attention,

only to see if they

remind me of you.

I go through the motions

but I already know

my choice will be no.

How can I give

myself to someone

when my heart

will always

be yours?

xcviii.

As I beg you to stay

eyes filled with tears,

silent confirmation of all my fears.

You'll fade into the past

like so many before you.

A repeating pattern;

no, no one stays.

As my body crumples

and agony sets in,

my mind reignites

the war I was in.

Unwillingly I face

my own heart,

in a battle to love me

that I didn't

start.

xcix.

The first time I lost you

my heart dropped further

than she ever had before.

The second time I lost you

she sunk just as deeply.

Yet now I've lost count

of the times we've said goodbye.

I've become an expert

in the art

of being

your ex.

c.
I can count the days now,
soon it will number
greater than the
fingers on both of my hands.
I feel proud of me now,
and how I've carried
myself from that hell to today,
somehow contently feeling everything.
It's been seven. Tomorrow
it will be eight.
Then nine. Ten.
And eleven.
Days without your voice.
Without your smile.
Your laugh.
Days without your texts.
Without your hugs.
Your lips.
Eleven will multiply
so quickly.
And though I've never
been much for math,
somehow it adds up to freedom.
It adds up to peace.
It adds up to
loving myself
the way I deserve.

ci.

At times I wonder

if I should approach you

as if a teacher,

so I can learn how to

close my heart off

and maintain your

cold, careless,

callous stance

with the feelings

of others.

At times I wonder,

but then realize,

how little I'd

wish to be

like you.

For I love far too

fiercely to ever

stoop so

low.

cii.

Today I release you.

I release you from

daily communication

and contact.

I release you from

the future dreams I

had for us.

I release you from

holding my body tightly

against yours.

I release you from

our chemistry and

our passion.

I release you from

the grip my love has

you under.

I release you from

my mind and

my heart.

My love, today I release you.

May this freedom from us

bring you the life without

me you appear

to want.

ciii.

There I was,

pouring all my energy,

my thoughts,

my spirit

into you.

And there you were,

soaking it all up

until I had nothing

left to give.

And I cannot imagine now

that you were deserving

of one moment

of it.

civ.

And oh my darling,

how you meant everything to me.

But I—

I meant nothing to you.

cv.

Today I learned

that you still could not

utter those three words

my soul yearns to hear.

Ever so quickly

you pour dozens of sentences

into the quiet,

yet none of it

fills my cup.

I am left to wonder

once again.

cvi.

I hush my own voice

and urge her to quiet.

We will make this work.

I hold on tightly

to you,

while I release my

grip on myself.

I watch idly as she falls,

the fear in her eyes

burned into memory.

But make no effort

to save me.

Hush now child,

you only need him.

You need nothing else

to survive.

Your love for him

is enough.

So quiet that voice

and be

satisfied.

Hush.

cvii.

All this time

I was searching for

a love that felt

like home,

and I found you,

and my soul just knew

her search was over.

Only you kept the

door closed,

not allowing me in.

Now somehow my soul

has given up,

abandoned her search.

For she shall not

have the capacity

to find home

in another.

cviii.

Sitting here unwillingly

playing the waiting game

for you.

I wait and wait

and love you

while I do.

You stall and stall

and make excuses

while I do.

Never have I felt

so torn

between what

my heart wants

and what

my mind fears.

Still, I remain

sitting here unwillingly

playing the waiting game

for you.

cix.

I hand you my heart

again and again.

You play with it for awhile.

I guess some men get

bored of playing

with the same toy.

No matter how hard I try.

No matter how deeply I cry.

I can never seem

to stop your

goodbye.

cx.

I've become a broken record,

forever attempting to play

our love song,

while you callously

skip over it.

cxi.

A hard truth:

they create time and space

for that which they love.

Sweet girl, do not settle

for anything less.

cxii.

You're becoming

a silhouette

in my memory.

Your face losing shape,

your smile now gone,

your skin only darkness.

You're a shadow

of what once

flooded my

brain.

cxiii.

You must find

a way through this

sweet child.

You have the moon

at your fingertips,

the stars within

your grasp.

Do not let one

man remove it

all from your

hands.

You will find

a way

out.

cxiv.
As if an open book,
I lay my pages out
for you,
hundreds of them
strewn about
for your perusal.
I knew
you may glance
at one or two
but might never
study them all.
I try to keep them
on display in hopes
your interest
may return.
Yet they lay there,
unexamined,
an open book
without a reader.

cxv.

You will never love me,

for your mind is too focused

on everything and everyone else.

While mine is busy writing about

all the ways I love you,

yours is busy creating all

the excuses you cannot.

Yet why is it that when all is

said and done,

I feel sorry for you?

For what is life

without love?

What will you be

without me?

A mishmash of

regret and

loneliness.

Yet you will never love me,

and one day I will learn

to stop.

cxvi.

I try to justify how you

make the choice,

to take solace

in my arms,

to indulge

in my body,

and yet

to not love me.

While I express

my love to you

again and again,

you keep returning,

yet never offering

me the same.

Confusion sinks into

my fractured heart

who relentlessly choses

you, a man

who does not love me.

What good can come

from that?

cxvii.

Loving you has become an endless battle.

My sturdy sword forged of pure love against yours,

forged of pure antipathy.

Yet, no matter how hard they clash,

my heart continuously endures death

from your blow.

cxviii.

As we drift and distance grows,

remember my love

it was you, for me.

It was always you.

cxix.

Like petals I will pluck

you one-by-one from my brain.

He loves me, he loves me not.

Each will flutter

and fall to the ground.

Oh child, he loves you not.

The petals lay still on the floor

wilting quietly

as I stand and leave.

He is now cleared from my mind,

and liberation like an empty

garden awaits me

to plant new seeds.

Oh, this feeling of

freedom.

I can finally feel myself

able to smile again.

Blooming.

Free of you.

I grow.

cxx.

How part of me

fears that I will

miss you

until my dying day,

when my

hands are weathered,

my frame used up

and my spirit

floating away.

She shall leave

my body behind,

but shall carry her

love for you

into whatever

lies beyond

anyway.

Perhaps

in the next life

we will get it right

and stay.

cxxi.

My girl,

how foolishly you gift yourself

and your heart to

someone who does

not deserve you.

All of that light my child!

All of that love!

How powerfully

it grows inside

of you.

Longing for a

soulmate,

a twin flame,

an eternal partner

to grasp a firm hold of you

and never

let go.

Be patient sweet one.

It is not him.

It is not him.

cxxii.

The words

spill onto paper

just as

blood pours from my veins:

Is this what he wanted?

To witness me bare everything

while his greedy eyes

soak it all in.

I watch as he laps up

every drop

of emotion

from my lifeless body

hanging on

paper before

him.

Only then he tightly

closes the

pages.

It is finished.

I am finished.

cxxiii.

So here it will stay.

My final thoughts on paper.

My final poem about you.

I sit and I wonder how many

times I cross your mind

in a day.

I want to ask, but I won't.

I sit and I wonder how many

times you start to type me

a message since we last spoke.

I want to ask, but I won't.

My brain accepts your absence

as if she has known all along

that you could not love me.

My heart, god my heart,

she is forever stubbornly alight

and aglow with all the ideas,

all the ways we could

make it right.

She speaks to me nightly

of how she wishes

your arms were pulling my body

tightly into yours.

She speaks to me nightly
of how she wishes
your name would light up
on my phone,
and she speaks to me nightly
of the hurt, begging me to heal her
from the hole where you once were.
As if to calm her ache
I've left your photo beside my bed,
a Band-Aid for her pain.
I sit. And I sit. And I wonder.
God how often I wonder
about you.
Maybe I always will.
Yet this will be my last poem.
My last reminiscing
of our time together.
I'll close this book,
our chapter finished,
and whisper
one final goodbye
to you,
my love.

FOUR.

I LOVE YOU

cxxiv.

A look. A touch. A kiss.

And it stops.

Ever so quickly.

My heart.

And for that moment.

One. Unforgettable. Moment.

I am yours.

A thousand years

could not erase it.

As it will be

whispered by

the universe herself.

Lightly spoken

in gentle wisps of wind.

In the bright shining of stars.

How a girl

fell for a boy

and nothing

else mattered.

cxxv.

In the expanse of

the universe,

with all its mysteries,

what a marvel it is

that she led

you to me.

cxxvi.

The soul of a wanderer

who never had a home,

yet I find all my maps

are ending at you.

As if the journey across continents

is fruitless when my roots have

finally become settled.

My fingertips travel across your body;

like distant roads, your scars lead me

on a sacred pilgrimage.

Dust off my weary feet,

at last, I am

where I

belong.

cxxvii.

And as the moon

I do all I can

to guide light

to the

darkest of nights.

And as I

drift on,

I call to you,

my sun.

Forever just out

of reach,

to light up

my sky

once more.

Forever apart.

Yet forever

within

my heart.

cxxviii.

You are entirely

nothing short of

everything

to me.

cxxix.
Of all the faces
I've seen and admired,
my mind lands on yours
most often.
Your features are
melded firmly into
memory;
so much so that I
dare say nothing
could remove you.
Of all the faces
I've yet to see and adore,
I can't help but imagine
yours will be the sight
I'll always wish to see
once more.
Endlessly and irreplaceably
present in my
mind's eye.

cxxx.

Millions of blossoms

lined the thin walls,

cloaking the nervousness.

And your blue,

it shone so bright.

Your smile

cast such a light.

That sun

danced upon your hair,

wisps of grey

sparkled.

Oh how

I've missed

you.

cxxxi.

Let's explore our

memories

you and I,

nostalgically

reverting to our

youth.

Kiss me for the

first time

once more,

as we bathe in

our renewed

innocence.

cxxxii.

The moon won't betray us,

the stars won't make a fuss.

Erase my memories of pain,

as I have tried so hard in vain.

Console me with that mouth,

explore my body further south.

Tell our story with these moans,

feel you deep within my bones.

Cleanse my soul with your tongue,

all those harmful words that stung.

Lick away my salty tears,

inside me we'll face our fears.

So, sink deeper still my darling,

our journeys just beginning.

cxxxiii.

The darkness in me

seems to complement

the darkness in you,

as if our shadows

secretly collided

and merged into

one.

cxxxiv.

He calls me his sunflower

and how eagerly I wish

to blossom for him.

To radiantly blush

in a thousand golden

tones of

yellow

for only him

to see.

cxxxv.

How will I know

their love is real?

When my body feels

calm in their presence.

When my nervous system

is at peace.

When the butterflies

are only ever-so-gently

present.

When he makes me feel

like I've come

home.

Only then will I know

it's real love.

cxxxvi.

Let me strip myself down

for you.

Layer by layer

I will unearth

my truth.

My roots.

My core.

Naked, I am fear.

I am hurt.

I am anger.

I am pain.

Stop me from covering it up

for you.

Layer by layer

allow me to reveal

and heal

it all.

cxxxvii.

Together

we sit under the moon,

as she pulls in the tide,

and our love

comes with it.

cxxxviii.

In an instant

you are all I see.

As if the world stopped moving

and all the people disappeared

and there was only you.

How magnetic it felt,

like you were born to find me,

and I you.

As if you became my sun

and my entire world

revolved around your warmth.

As if the force of gravity

had pulled us into one another

and now we are here,

magnetically gravitating towards each other.

And if the epitome of life is this,

then I am forever and completely

satisfied.

cxxxix.

Give me rainforests,

salty seas,

endless summer,

freshly grown food

from Mother Earth

and your hand.

I've come to find

this is all I'll

ever need.

cxl.

If we found ourselves

separated

at opposite ends of this earth

my love,

I would trek a mile in moments,

scale mountains in minutes,

cross seas in a day,

all to be close

to you

again.

cxli.

Sunlight slipping gently inside the curtains

as I wake to the muted sound of ocean waves;

curled up in pillows, a silky duvet

and you.

All of my favourite mornings are made up

of this.

cxlii.

If we ever get there,

to the end of this world,

if tomorrow will not come

and if our time here is now done,

my darling, my sweet love,

all I'll ask of you

is that we let it

crumble around us

as it is bound to do.

But hold onto me,

please don't look away.

This world can meet its end,

yet our love will stay.

cxliii.

Was there even life

before I met you?

I cannot remember now

as it feels as though

I had been trapped

in a grey cloud

of misery.

Was there even love

before I met you?

I cannot remember now

as it feels as though

I have never felt

this type of love

before you.

How eternally grateful I am

for this life,

for this love,

for you.

cxliv.

Perhaps if I split my heart open

and let you look around,

then you'll finally see

there's only you to be found.

I love and want

only you.

cxlv.

I yearn for a love

that feels like coming home.

Home, a mythical place,

lost, yet never found,

an imaginary vision

I forever pursue.

cxlvi.

What is it

about you

that makes me

want to be a

better woman

and push myself

to accomplish

every goal I have

ever had?

You are my

motivation,

my love,

and I know

together

we could

find forever.

cxlvii.

Our lips met today

as they had

a hundred times before.

Your skin touched mine today

as it had

a thousand times before.

Yet my heart

she continues to race,

beating as if

this was new to her.

As if she has never seen

or felt

or loved

in such a way.

Feebly, my

mind tries to tame her

but she runs

wild at the thought

of you.

cxlviii.

To feel so alive

when I am with you

that I fear

nothing else in this world

will ever compare.

To feel so alive

when I am with you

that I know

my heart could never

replicate this.

You bring me to life

in all the ways

I've ever wanted.

So, sit with me

under this midnight sky

and come

alive with me

my love.

cxlix.

Perhaps there is a

deeper purpose,

a deeper meaning

within

our connection

that pushes then pulls.

Seemingly inescapable.

Back together

we stand once more.

Perhaps there is a

deeper purpose,

and I am to teach

you to open

your heart

and love,

and you are to teach

me to let go

of my fears

and live each

moment

in joy.

cl.

Indulge with me.

Caress me with your words.

Get lost with me.

We shall burn together

in passion

forever.

cli.
As my belly hungers
for food,
my heart hungers
for you.
Won't you make me
a meal of your
love?
I shall feast
without ceasing,
forever nourished
with only
you.

clii.

Sleepily my arms find you

in the darkness,

and without opening our eyes

we pull the other in close.

Skin on skin.

Hands running through your hair,

gentle kisses on your cheek.

Bodies warming the other

while we drift off together

in peaceful embrace.

Oh, how I love

dreamy nights

with you.

cliii.

Will you travel with me

back in time?

Before social media.

Before cell phones.

So we can live in

the present moment,

without distraction

and focus our energy

on simply being alive.

Experiencing each moment

without a photo,

without a like,

and just exist

together

you and I.

cliv.
The currents of passion
race through my veins
collecting in my centre,
explosions surge
to the surface.
My skin is now
flush with residue
of you.
All is unclear
except one thing.
I want you now.
Want you, now.
My limbs ache for the
frenzied ecstasy
you pour over them.
It's almost more than
I should take,
but more is all I ask.
Don't stop.
More.
The verge of
perfection,
the gateway
to heaven on earth
is this,
it must be
this.

clv.
My heart is beating
stronger than before.
My mouth is full of you.
The walls are falling
all around me,
you taste of honeydew.
An escape so violent
but pain still lingers.
I'll never stop wanting.
I'll never stop needing.
So I close my eyes,
drink you in,
and drop by drop
I'll swallow down
any piece I can,
so you stay with
me in some way.

clvi.

Today I thought of you

just as I do

each and every day.

The outline of your figure

lingering in my mind.

The way your breath changed

as you slept next to me.

How my body fits perfectly against

your chest in embrace.

And with every thought

my mind softens

as she succumbs to

the delicacy of her love

for you.

My darling,

it is always

and only

you.

clvii.

Think of me

when the sun rises

and bathes the sleepy earth

with her rays.

Think of me

when the sun sets

and her bright light

returns to her.

Think of me

when the moon glows

softly and gently

in the night.

Think of me

all the times

in between,

just as I find

myself thinking

of you.

FIVE.

HEALING

clviii.

I am learning

to love myself.

My flaws are not who I am.

My insecurities abound,

yet I stand before you

fighting back.

And I love me.

I love my imperfections

for they have built me

from the ground up.

I love my weaknesses

for within them

I have learned my strengths.

And I stand before you,

whole. Worthy.

Human

and loved.

clix.

Perhaps I'm stronger than I seem,

an emotional warrior

who has risen from every

beating she has received.

Perhaps I'm more resilient than I think,

able to withstand the widest

ranges of highs and lows.

Yet maybe I simply

want to be weak

for a day.

Maybe my body merely wants to rest,

as if laying in a peaceful meadow

with bright blue skies,

singing songbirds and

the warm shining sun.

Maybe my soul

wishes to put her armour

down and relax.

Perhaps I'm stronger than I seem.

But will you lay with me

awhile sweet one,

in the glory

of our weakness?

clx.

I've never been that girl,

the one with countless friends,

flawless skin,

perfect parents,

and a healthy childhood.

I've never been her

and I think if I had

perhaps I would never have

experienced emotional depth,

fierce self-pride for

my strength and recovery,

or even learned

how to love people correctly.

I've never been her,

and I think if I had

perhaps my passion for

writing, for poetry,

for honesty, for love,

may not exist

the same way.

So no, I've never been her,

but god am I glad

I am me.

clxi.

A reminder for you today

sweet soul:

drink your water,

move your body,

get outside.

And most importantly,

love.

Open that heart.

Never let this world harden it.

Love as loudly,

and fiercely,

and passionately

as you can.

And don't forget

to love yourself

along the way.

clxii.

They float by

like clouds

or bubbles

filled to the brim

with my emotions,

and I am finally learning

to allow them

to pass me by.

clxiii.

I choose me this time.

A different beginning.

A different middle.

A different end.

One that doesn't leave me crying

in puddles of tears on the floor.

This time I choose me.

This time I choose love.

The best kind of love—

My own.

clxiv.

Place your foot ever firmly

in my hands

and I shall lift you

one step higher.

Inching closer to

the clouds,

abandoning all

obstacles prior.

For we are only

going upwards

dear one.

Upwards towards life.

Towards each other.

Towards love.

Raise me up, as I will you.

Until we reside limitless

as angels in the

sky.

clxv.
Whenever you feel hopeless
and the pain will not ease,
my love, take a breath,
as deep into your belly
as you can.
Inhaling peace.
Exhaling negativity.
Inhaling light,
a light which fills you,
surrounds you,
with love.
Exhaling despair,
allowing it to leave
your body, it does
not belong there.
My love, keep breathing.
Deeply. Purposefully.
Cleanse yourself of the pain,
and embrace the peace
of the present moment.
For my child,
this too
shall pass.

clxvi.
I gaze at how small she was,
How petite. How sweet.
Yet how naive and how trusting.
I watched as she grew,
through one trauma and another.
A seemingly endless crash course
of life lessons.
And I watched as she took each
rock bottom she faced,
lifted her head and dried her tears,
giving up was not her option.
Even though there were times
the temptation of escape lingered.
No, not her. She fought.
Day after day after day.
A modern-day warrior,
who continued to choose love
despite it all.
Despite this cruel and broken world.
Chose love.
I gaze at how powerful I am.
How strong. How kind.
How courageous and how unique.
I watch as I grow.
And I am proud of her.
Of me.

clxvii.

My feet have never been

the type to stay put,

for they wish to carry me

to all the wonders I have

yet to see.

And though I may have lived

half my life and not yet

had the chance,

I can feel them

restless,

impatient,

longing.

Soon we shall go,

to see all the wonders,

exploring this world

ever wild

and free.

clxviii.

So I shall wait

for the universe

to bring me all that I

want, need

and deserve.

I will speak my

desires into existence

and allow it

to come to me,

like a butterfly flutters

to a flower.

I will no longer

try to force

or control;

my destiny shall

find me.

I am ready to

receive.

clxix.
Sweet girls of mine,
my heart could burst
exploring all the ways it loves you.
I'll hug you tight
and kiss you first,
smiling at your laugh,
oh, but I love you.
How fiercely I want
to protect you.
How fearlessly I will
battle for you.
Sweet girls of mine,
my heart is full,
joy overflows,
simply because
I love you.
Nothing can compare,
and nothing can replace you.
I offer you
a garden of my love,
forever green,
with flowers which
will never wilt,
and a sun that
will forever shine
for you,
sweet girls of mine.

clxx.

How quickly you've grown

into limitless young women

with the world waiting at your feet.

Always remember my dear loves,

be brave, take adventures

and be kind to all you meet.

clxxi.

I mimic a flower

and reach

my roots deeply

into Mother Earth.

I stretch

myself upwards

and open to

the sun.

I stay grounded

while lengthening

to the sky.

I am a flower.

Plant yourself

next to me

dear one,

and our garden

shall thrive.

clxxii.

My life's philosophy is

summarized by simply this:

love.

Our world needs a revolution

filled with it.

clxxiii.

It's taken me

so many years

for my mind, heart and soul

to realize that

the only love

I truly need

is my own.

clxxiv.

What do you deserve?

My sweet child,

you deserve the moon

lighting your nights.

You deserve the most

powerful of loves.

You deserve the magic

of an authentic soul.

What do you deserve?

My sweet child,

you deserve it all

and everything.

No more settling

for less.

clxxv.

You see my child

it will all work out.

It may be unclear,

it may take patience,

it may mean wading

through hurt and

an ocean of tears,

but you see, my sweet child,

you will reach the shore

once more,

and all will be well.

It will all work out.

No matter how many

times you return

to the depths.

clxxvi.

Keep your money.

Keep your things.

Keep your shallow ideals.

For all they are

is a prison

of our modern world.

Keep it all,

and I will offer

you my sympathy.

I shall keep

only that which

ignites my soul.

Give me ocean.

Give me sunlight.

Give me forests.

Give me freedom.

Give me peace.

And I shall

be forever

flooded with

true wealth.

clxxvii.

Give me a taste

of adventure,

daring, exhilarating

and a little bit mad,

intentionally placed

in the present,

so I may

return to the

fountain of

my youth.

clxxviii.

I can see it

as if I was present

in this moment.

Sand filling the space

between my toes.

Warm, gentle sea water

gliding and flowing

over my skin.

I can taste it.

The salt in the air.

Smell it.

Tropical flora

filling my nose.

Don't open my eyes,

just leave me here

to escape

in my mind,

as I sit here,

legs folded,

alone in my

room.

clxxix.

You are safe.

How heavily these words

fall on ears that have

only known chaos.

What a foreign concept

safety can be.

Breathe deeply.

Lean into it,

sweet child.

You. Are. Safe.

And by right

you deserve

to be so.

clxxx.

Rest your weary eyes,

let the heaviness

sink in.

You've made it

so far

sweet one.

For now

it is done.

Still the shaking

in your body,

you have

permission

to let go.

Now rest. Rest. Rest.

Just so.

clxxxi.

Is it truly a thing

to fear?

To be still,

at peace,

alone,

in darkness?

I am learning

to find comfort

in those moments

in life.

Why should I fear them

in death?

clxxxii.

There are days

when the emotional turmoil

inside my body

appears to rest.

These are the days

when I become silently numb

to it all.

I wonder, however, if this is

truly rest,

or if I simply need

to shut down

and no longer process

anymore.

clxxxiii.

There is power in vulnerability:

the power of awareness,

the power to heal.

My love, it is time to take your power back.

clxxxiv.

If you're ever feeling

lonely my love,

step outside.

Feel Mother Earth

on your bare feet,

ponder how she nourishes

your living body from

her soil.

Listen to the birds

singing brightly in the trees,

filling your ears with

their music as it blends

in with the wind.

Look up at the sky

as the sun smiles down on you,

or at night when the beaming stars

draw pictures in constellations

for you to find.

You are never truly alone

sweet child,

for life

and love

surround you.

clxxxv.

Accepting living in the grey,

not needing all the answers,

not demanding black and white.

Letting it go so I can exist

in a space of not knowing,

and learn to find

peace here.

clxxxvi.

I gaze down,

another blank page

before me,

pure and untarnished,

open for me

to fill.

As I watch my hand moving,

the ink leaving the pen,

I feel release.

As if with every stroke

I can breathe

a little easier,

soften a little deeper,

think a little clearer.

All I need are

blank pages

before me.

Magic does

the rest.

clxxxvii.

How she has carried me

across a battlefield

of judgements.

Near misses and straight hits.

Yet somehow always lives on.

I pause and contemplate

how I should thank her,

when I myself

started this war.

Every so gently,

hand over heart,

I pledge my love.

Marital vows to myself.

To protect her

for as long

as we both

shall live.

clxxxviii.

Take caution

with your beliefs my love

for your heart

shall feed you lies,

and the mind

—she'll pick and chose

what she believes

is right.

Sweet girl be careful.

Religion will blind you

and his love will poison

your heart.

Church and this man,

from these things

turn away.

clxxxix.
Then there are some losses
which are not a loss.
Oh, you'll feel it. The pain.
It will ache all over your
entire body and though
you feel like death shall
come for you …
you'll awaken the next
morning.
And the next. And the next.
Each day will be different.
One day
weightless.
One day heavy.
Yet the sun, she will
remind you that
there is light, endless light,
that will shine
for you.
Seek the light
my darling.
For she is ever present.
Ever shining.
As are you.

cxc.

You are enough.

How many times

I've heard these words,

yet they seem to fall

on my indifferent ears.

You are enough.

As I attempt to absorb them

somehow an overwhelming urge

to collapse into tears emerges.

You are enough.

What makes their acceptance

so difficult, so alien?

As if it's being spoken

in a language unknown.

You. Are. Enough.

I repeat it quietly to myself.

You deserve to be loved.

You deserve to be safe.

My child, you are, and

always were,

enough.

cxci.

Though I feel I did not have a home

that loved me unconditionally,

there are some things I've found

feel like home, nonetheless.

It feels like home

when I sip my morning coffee

each day.

It feels like home

when I sit by my open window

while the breeze blows in.

It feels like home

when I hear my daughters' laughter

within these walls.

It feels like home

when I am wrapped up safely

within your arms.

A house can be a home

when all you love is within it,

and when you know for certain

you would never abandon it.

That is home

to me.

cxcii.

When the hurt and tears

are replaced by

anger you will

have taken that first

step in healing.

And when the anger

is replaced by

peace you will

have finally come to a place

where you can heal.

Heal yourself sweet one.

You deserve that

and so much more.

cxciii.

Today is brightly aglow

with promise

and shines of rebirth.

My storm is at its calmest,

whispering of revival.

Watch me be born again

into who I was always

meant to be.

You'll sing praises of pride

for the girl who

almost died

but was born again

as herself.

Free her

and I shall be her

for all eternity.

cxciv.

What would success look like

to me?

To make a difference.

To leave a mark.

To soften a heart.

To change a mind.

To create freedom.

To spread love.

If I can accomplish one of these,

I'll fade eternally away

in content.

cxcv.

Welcome to my perfect storm.

If you've come to cry,

I'll hold you.

Sit tight in these

little arms,

I'll accept you as you are.

Darling there is no

picture perfect,

there is no greener grass.

We all carry battle scars,

we all have a past.

So close those

tired, tearful eyes,

dear one,

I will be here.

Though love was lost,

I remain yours.

This heart,

these hands,

will hold

you.

cxcvi.

You are a beacon of light,

illuminating this gloom

which I am

submerged in.

How grateful I am

to each of you

who hold space

for the darkest parts

of me.

Who reveal the truth,

that I am not alone.

Who demonstrate

the restorative power

of friendship.

My sweet supporters,

how unconditionally

I love you.

cxcvii.
One thing to remember
sweet ones,
is never rush your healing.
For the quicker you attempt it,
the quicker you may stumble.
Savour it.
Bathe your very
soul within its
self-preserving waters.
Allow your healing
to sink into your
every atom.
And only then,
wish the excuses goodbye,
the old you farewell.
For you are going to emerge
from this self-love period
as the most powerful,
authentic version
of you imaginable.
So no, do not rush it sweet child;
allow it.

cxcviii.
Your first breath
meant the
beginning of my life,
the beginning
of my
beginning.
You changed me
entirely
and I am yours
in everyway.
My limbs move
for you.
My heart beats
for you.
My soul enlightens
for you.
In all I do or
ever will
you are my first
thought
and my last.
My darling girls, you are
all and you are
everything
to me.

cxcix.

Let me collect your smiles

and place them

in a jar,

so whenever you are sad

I can bring it

to you and

remind you of the joy you

felt not

so long ago.

When your heart is

breaking, I will

present them

and help you mend,

putting its pieces

back together again.

I've saved them all for

you, your smiles;

how they

shine like sunset

at dusk.

cc.

I will no longer sit complacent

and witness my life passing by.

No. I will choose to create the one

I want: a life full of adventure

and wonder.

Let them

watch as I finally

choose me.

cci.

Hope.

I hold it gently against my chest,

faded and grey.

Its edges have worn,

softly frayed.

I feel its heart still beating.

Slowly, silently.

A rhythmic melody

of quiet conviction.

ccii.

I believe we are like wildflowers

you and I,

for we adapt and grow so beautifully

no matter where we've ended up.

cciii.
Looking for my balance
as if my life is a spinning top;
I seem to always teeter
to the right
or to the left.
Leaning too far one way
or the other,
desperate to stay upright.
Still, I realise
that tipping over
is okay, it's allowed.
It's human.
Life spins so quickly,
we cannot always
remain on our axis.
Give yourself permission
to tilt, to fall,
to collapse.
You are human.
As am I.
Our balance,
though imperfect,
will return
once again.

cciv.

My darling,

your capability

is not defined

by your illness.

No, my love,

it is defined by

your persistence.

Your resolution.

Your purposefulness.

Your courage.

And I, for one,

believe in

you.

ccv.
How many ways are there
to express that this is the end?
The end of this part,
this chapter,
this book of wounds
which I've compiled
as a witness to
my broken heart.
The end of this season,
this story,
this pain.
You may believe
that closing a page
is merely that.
But my loves,
it represents so much more.
Here ends this part of me,
a part I hid from so many.
A part I never chose.
A part that has served its purpose
and I can now let go.
It has ended.
My everlasting wish for you
is that your pain
ends too.

ccvi.

They ask me why.

Why expose it?

Why continue?

As if the answer

is to simply bury myself.

But if I

can touch

one heart, one soul.

And if they no

longer

feel alone in this broken world.

And if they can find

peace

in sharing my innermost thoughts.

This is why. And so.

I write.

I write.

I write.

Let's find our happiness sweet ones.

From my heart to yours.

Much love,

Jess

www.ingramcontent.com/pod-product-compliance
Lightning Source LLC
Chambersburg PA
CBHW051513120626
46551CB00012B/907